Helen Keller
Inspiring Opportunity for All

by Jennifer Marino Walters
illustrated by Scott R. Brooks

Red Chair Press   Egremont, Massachusetts

Look! Books are produced and published by Red Chair Press:

Red Chair Press LLC   PO Box 333   South Egremont, MA 01258-0333

www.redchairpress.com

 FREE lesson guide at www.redchairpress.com/free-activities

Publisher's Cataloging-In-Publication Data
(Provided by Cassidy Cataloguing Services, Inc.)
Names: Marino Walters, Jennifer, author. | Brooks, Scott R., illustrator.
Title: Helen Keller : inspiring opportunity for all / by Jennifer Marino Walters ;
illustrated by Scott R. Brooks.
Other titles: Look! books (Red Chair Press). Beginner biography

Description: Egremont, Massachusetts : Red Chair Press, [2024] | Includes
    index. | Interest age level: 006-009. | Summary: Helen Keller is an
    American author and educator who was blind and deaf. Even though she
    could not see or hear like most people, she finished college and became a
    writer and speaker for others with these disabilities. There seemed to be
    nothing Helen could not do.--Publisher.

Identifiers: ISBN: 9781643712482 (library hardcover) | 9781643712543
    (softcover) | 9781643712604 (ebook) | LCCN: 2022943805

Subjects: LCSH: Keller, Helen, 1880-1968--Juvenile literature. | Women
    authors, American--20th century--Biography--Juvenile literature. |
    Deafblind people--United States--Biography-- Juvenile literature. | Human
    rights workers--United States--Biography--Juvenile literature. | CYAC:
    Keller, Helen, 1880-1968. | Women authors, American--20th century-
    -Biography. | Deafblind people--Biography. | Human rights workers--
    United States--Biography. | LCGFT: Biographies. | BISAC: JUVENILE
    NONFICTION / Biography & Autobiography / Women. | JUVENILE
    NONFICTION / Biography & Autobiography / Social Activists. | JUVENILE
    NONFICTION / Disabilities & Special Needs.

Classification: LCC: HV1624.K4 M37 2024 | DDC: 362.4/1092--dc23

Photo credits: p. 13, 14, 21, 22, 24: Library of Congress

Printed in the United States of America

0324 1P CGF24

Table of Contents

Mysterious Illness

Helen Keller was born on June 27, 1880 in Tuscumbia, Alabama. When she was 1.5 years old, she got very sick. Her illness caused her to lose both her sight and hearing.

Helen began to communicate using signs she made up. But when she realized her family communicated with their mouths and not with signs, she became very angry. Helen often kicked and screamed.

A Special Teacher

Things began to change when Helen was 6. That's when her parents hired a teacher named Anne Sullivan to help her learn. Helen resisted at first. She hit, punched, and kicked Anne.

But Anne remained patient. She did not give up on Helen. And finally, Helen began to listen to her.

Good to Know

Helen once wrote, "The most important day I remember in all my life is the day my teacher, Anne Mansfield Sullivan, came to me."

Learning Language

Anne began to teach Helen words through finger spelling. The first word Helen learned was "doll." Another was "water." To teach Helen "water," Anne placed one of Helen's hands under a waterspout and spelled out W-A-T-E-R in Helen's other hand. Helen then repeated the word in Anne's hand.

Within a few months, Helen had a **vocabulary** of hundreds of words.

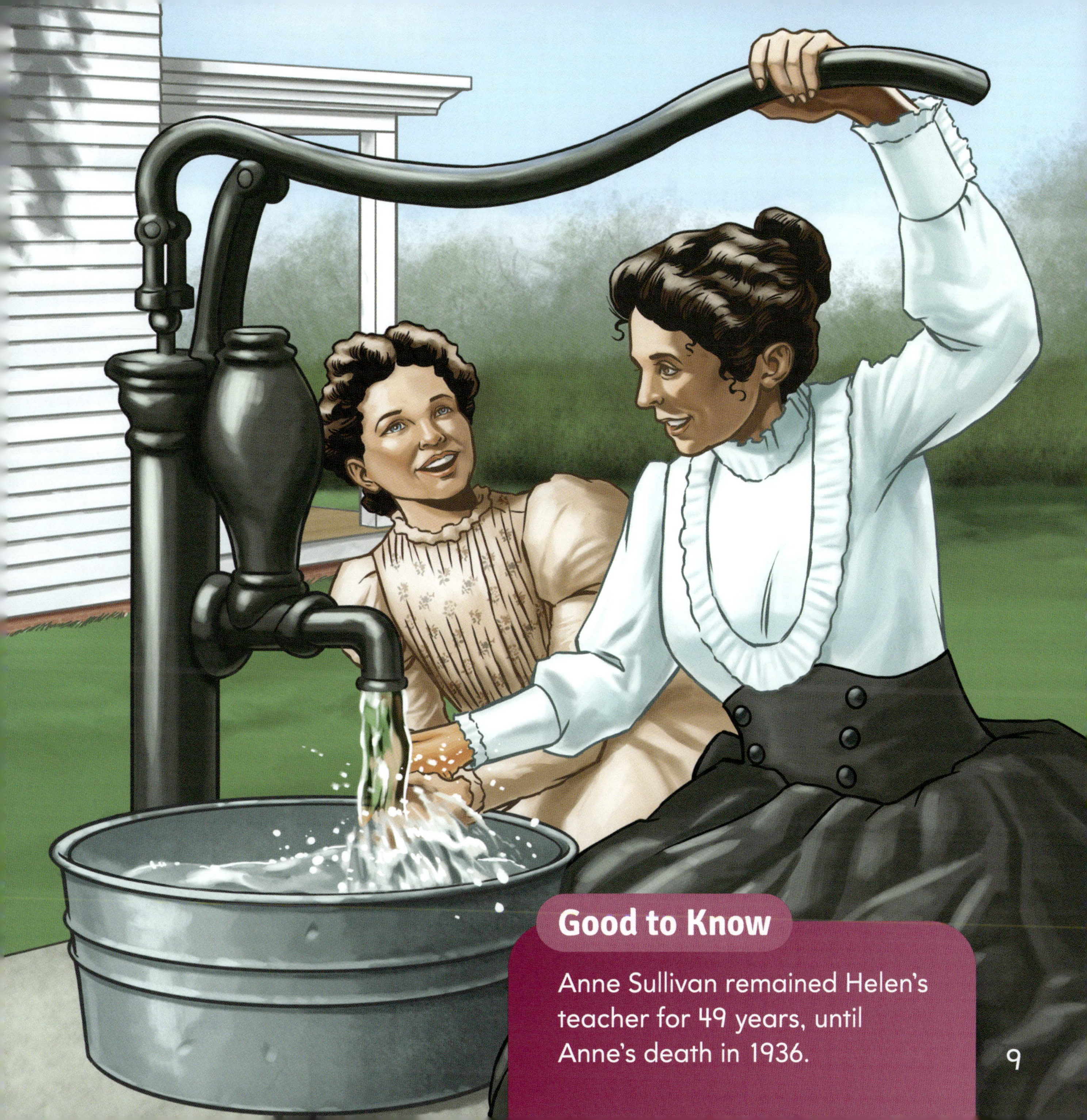

Good to Know

Anne Sullivan remained Helen's teacher for 49 years, until Anne's death in 1936.

9

Anne also taught Helen to read **Braille** and to print block letters. At age 9, Helen began learning to read lips by touching people's mouths to feel their speech movements. She also began taking speech classes at the Horace Mann School for the Deaf in Massachusetts.

After 25 years of hard work, Helen was able to speak well enough that people could understand her.

An Education

In 1896, Helen enrolled in the Cambridge School for Young Ladies to prepare for college. Her dream college, Harvard University, did not accept women at the time. So, Helen enrolled in Radcliffe College in Massachusetts in 1899. Anne attended classes with her and finger-spelled what the teachers said.

Many people believed it was impossible for a deaf and blind person to go to college. But Helen proved them wrong. She graduated with honors in 1904 at age 24. That made her the first blind and deaf person to ever earn a college degree.

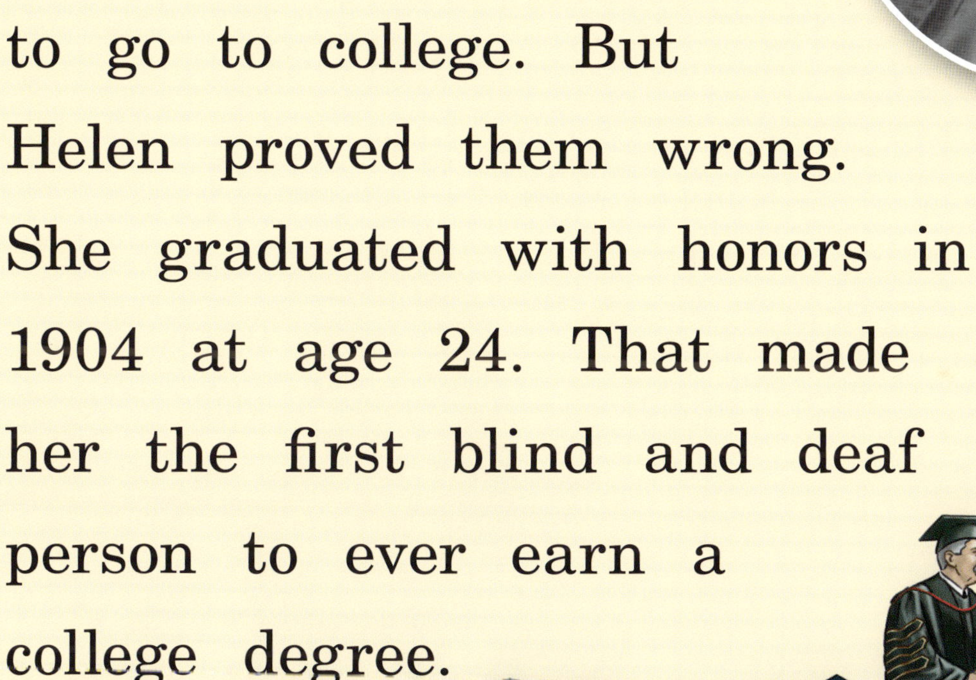

Helping Others

After college, Helen set out
to improve the lives of others
with **disabilities**. She spoke to
audiences about her experiences.
She worked to raise
money and support
for blind people.

In 1926, Helen met with
President Calvin Coolidge to
talk to him about people like her.

In 1915, Helen
helped begin Helen
Keller International
to support the blind and
to fight hunger. She also
helped start the American Civil
Liberties Union (ACLU) in 1920
to defend and protect the rights
of all people.

The Right to Vote

Helen also fought for women's rights. She spoke at public meetings to demand that women get paid equally as men. She also worked to get women the right to vote.

On August 18, 1920, the 19th **Amendment** to the U.S. Constitution was signed into law. It officially gave women the right to vote. But Helen didn't stop there.

VOTES FOR WOMEN
VOTE "YES" NOVE
THE CALL
3 CENTS
FIVE P.
FINAL HOME
U.S. WOMEN GET VOTE
Korea Plot Against U.S. Solons
26 Million Win Right to Vote by Tennessee Action
HELEN KELLER RIDING IN GREAT PARADE OF SUFFRAGISTS IN BOSTON CAMPAIGN
VOTES FOR WOMEN
VOTES FOR WOMEN

Worldwide Travels

Helen was not only a good speaker. She also wrote countless articles and 12 books using Braille or a typewriter.

As she got older, she did not slow down. From 1946 to 1957, Helen traveled to 35 countries to speak and **advocate** for the blind. At age 75, she took a 40,000-mile trip across Asia.

TWA

An Inspiration

Helen was elected to the Women's Hall of Fame in 1965. Three years later, she died at age 87 on June 1, 1968.

Helen continues to
be an inspiration to
millions of people,
especially those
with disabilities. Her
achievements are proof
that with hard work and
determination, people
can overcome any obstacle.
And that nothing should
hold a person back.

Helen with a
young fan in 1965.

Timeline: Big Dates in Helen's Life

1880: Helen is born in Tuscumbia, Alabama.

1882: Helen gets a sickness that causes her to lose her sight and hearing.

1887: Anne Sullivan becomes Helen's teacher. She begins teaching Helen words through finger spelling.

1890: Helen starts speech classes to learn how to talk.

1904: She graduates with honors from Radcliffe College in Massachusetts.

1915: Helen co-founds Helen Keller International.

1920: She co-founds the American Civil Liberties Union (ACLU).

1964: Helen is awarded the Presidential Medal of Freedom.

1965: She is elected to the Women's Hall of Fame.

1968: Helen dies in her sleep at age 87.

Anne Sullivan, left, with Helen in 1914.

Words to Know

advocate: to support or argue for something or someone

Amendment: a change to the Constitution

Braille: a system of writing for blind people that uses raised dots for touching

determination: continuing to try to do something that is hard

disabilities: physical or mental conditions that limit a person's movements, senses, or activities

vocabulary: the words that make a language

Learn More at the Library

(Check out these books to read with others.)

Berne, Emma Carlson. *What's Your Story, Helen Keller?* Lerner, 2016.

Keller, Helen. *The Story of My Life.* Dover Publications, 1996.

Platt, Christine. *The Story of Helen Keller.* Rockridge Press, 2020.

Thompson, Gare. *Who Was Helen Keller?* Penguin Workshop, 2003.

Index

Helen reading
Braille at age 27.

About the Author

Jennifer Marino Walters and her husband live with their twin boys and daughter in the Washington D.C. area. She is grateful to have role models of determination like Helen Keller for her children.